Finn MacCool and Big Head MacTavish

A legend retold by Martin Waddell

Illustrated by Johanna Boccardo

GW01551151

Chapter 1

There once was an Irish giant named Finn MacCool, and a Scottish giant called Big Head MacTavish.

Big Head went round boasting that he could beat up any other giant there ever was. He did finish off a few of the smaller ones. Great Green Gorman from Grimsby, Big Mike from Orkney and Three-Headed John from Cornwall all came along, one after the other.

BIFF went MacTavish,
and Gorman was gone.

BANG went MacTavish,
and Big Mike was laid flat.

BONG BONG BONG

went MacTavish (one
bong for each head).
That finished off
Three-Headed John.

"Who's next?" roared MacTavish.

"Finn MacCool," someone said. "MacCool who lives over the water, in Ireland."

"MacCool?" bellowed MacTavish. "Bring him on and I'll whack him one-handed."

MacTavish marched around, bragging about what he would do to this Finn MacCool.

"I'll bandy-leg Finn MacCool. I'll cross-eye and cook him. I'll buckle his belly and serve him with porridge!" MacTavish roared.

Now when you're built like a very small mountain and you roar a lot, word soon gets about. And it's not far from Scotland, where MacTavish lived, to Finn MacCool's home on the Antrim shore in Ireland. Finn heard every word…and he wasn't pleased.

He took a big rock and chucked it right over to Scotland. It knocked off MacTavish's bonnet and laid the Scottish giant out cold.

When MacTavish came round, there was the huge rock beside him. Tied to the rock was Finn's note:

To: B.H. MacTavish (Giant)

Come to Ireland and fight me.

F. MacCool (Giant).

Now, it was a very big rock and MacTavish wasn't stupid. Any giant who could throw a rock that size from Ireland to Scotland had to be REALLY, REALLY BIG.

"He *might* be as big as me," MacTavish thought cautiously.

So he wrote his own note and tied it to the rock. Then he hurled the rock back. **BONG!** The rock landed in Antrim, only just missing Finn's toe.

Finn read the note:

To: F. MACCOOL (SO-CALLED GIANT)
SORRY. CAN'T COME. THE IRISH SEA IS TOO DEEP TO PADDLE ACROSS AND I CAN'T SWIM. B.H. MACTAVISH (MUCH BIGGER GIANT THAN YOU).

"You're not getting out of it that easily!" roared Finn.

So he did the kind of thing giants do, when they want to impress people. He started to hack at the cliffs. When he'd finished, the cliffs were in a bad way, but he had made a rock bridge right over the sea to Scotland.

Some of Finn's bridge is still there on the Antrim coast. It is called the Giant's Causeway.

Then Finn tossed the big rock back to MacTavish, with another note:

To: B.H. MacTavish
(Big mouth).
No need for a swim.
I've built you a bridge
So you can walk over.
See you Saturday.
F. MacCool
(biggest giant there is).

MacTavish was so angry at being called Big Mouth, that he forgot about being cautious. He chucked the rock back with a note for Finn:

This time it was Finn's turn to be cautious. "Maybe he is bigger than me," Finn thought to himself. "I'd best have a plan, just in case."

Chapter 2

Saturday came, and Finn had everything ready.

Over Finn's bridge came MacTavish. He was so big that his shadow darkened the sea.

MacTavish roared, "Where's Finn MacCool?"

CLUMP. CLUMP. CLUMP.

Up popped Finn's wife, Mrs MacCool.

"Pardon me, Mr MacTavish," said Mrs MacCool. "Finn wants to fight you today, but he's been called away on urgent big business."

"What's that?" bellowed MacTavish. "I've come all this way and now Finn is not here to fight me?"

"Finn will be back soon," said Mrs MacCool. "He said maybe you'd come in the house for some tea, and wait there till he gets back."

"Well, maybe I will," said MacTavish, who was thirsty after all his clumping and roaring.

He stomped into the house.

"Mind now," said Mrs MacCool. "No roaring or you'll wake the baby."

"What baby?" said Giant MacTavish.

"Our baby," said Mrs MacCool. "Our wee Titch MacCool."

And she showed him the baby. (The baby was really Finn, dressed in huge baby clothes.)

"Gug-gug-gug!" cried the baby, waving his battle-axe rattle.

"Titch is still tiny," explained Mrs MacCool. "He's six months old and he just won't grow. But we're hoping that one day he'll be as big as his dad."

"Oh…er!" gurgled MacTavish.

"He's having a terrible time with his teeth," said Mrs MacCool. "Maybe you'd give him an old tree trunk to chew on?"

MacTavish gingerly held out a tree trunk, and Finn bit his thumb.

"AHHHHHH!" screamed MacTavish.

"You've upset my wee baby!" cried Mrs MacCool.

The Very Big Baby bounced out of his cot, waving his battle-axe rattle. Out of the house sprinted MacTavish, with the Very Big Baby hot on his heels. There was no time to make for the bridge.

SPLOOSH!

MacTavish dived into the water.

MacTavish swam over to Scotland as fast as he could. (He'd *lied* to Finn. He *could* swim.)

The Very Big Baby threw a huge rock after him.

GIANT'S CAUSEWAY

SCOTLAND

IRISH SEA

LOUGH NEAGH

NORTHERN IRELAND

ISLE OF MAN

The rock is still there, in the sea. It's called the Isle of Man. There was a hole left in the ground where Finn picked up the rock. It soon filled with water and now people call it Lough Neagh.

MacTavish never came back to fight Finn. When he reached Scotland, he scuttled off to the Highlands and hid in a cave near Inverness.

Some say MacTavish is hiding there still. He's afraid that one day Finn MacCool might come looking for him…Finn, or the Very Big Baby they call Titch MacCool.